DONE RIGHT

THE BOOK

By

Charles M. Day III

Standard copy right

ISBN# 978-1-257-03336-2

Dedicated to;

Rev. Charles M. Day his wife Mary Jane (Hale) Day,

Charles M. Day Jr. his wife Elizabeth Ann (Fortenberry) Day

As I grew up and met the world I faltered when I did it on my own. My actions were only successful only when I listened to those that had passed before me. Chief among them were my Grand Parents and Parents. The phrase that was drilled into my head that I could not, (or in some cases would not), understand until later in my life was "**It is done when all avenues are explored and problems repaired or fixed, no matter how long it takes**." The lessons they taught me are the reasons why I am writing this book.

ABOUT THE AUTHOR..

Charles M. day III was born in 1950 in Memphis Tennessee. He grew up in Clinton Mississippi. Married later in 1990 Charles has live for 21 years with his wife and has three children and one grandchild, At the time of this book. After serving 4 years in the US Navy as a Trained Aviation Electrician, Charles spent time with the family construction business learning every aspect of the business. Now Charles Is employed as a maintenance and warehouseman man for a large agronomy and grain company. He is also author of a book of poetry, THOUGHTS OF THE TRANSPLANTED MISSISSIPPIAN, and Charles is also writing a new book of short stories, "Fables from a Deep Fried Southerner". Charles writes in the style that teaches a lesson or showing up a problem he feels is needed to be pointed out.

DISCLAIMER

Charles Day dose not name the companies he works for or the names of the equipment manufactures to insure that no confidences are breached. However the company names are listed as reference at the end of this book.

THE BEGINNING

There where the two words that my Grand Parents and Parents did not like these were "IF" and "EXPEDIENCE". This was because of how people viewed and applied these words.

Encarta World English Dictionary defines "**Expedience**" as; **1. Use of short-term effective methods:** the use of methods that bring the most immediate benefits, based on practical rather than moral considerations

2. Appropriateness: the usefulness, appropriateness, or advisability of something, especially of a particular action or type of behavior in a particular situation

"Doubts about the expediency of such a course in the present crisis"

The problem is that in today's thinking this definition is out dated. The definition of Expedience for the last 20 or so years till now is. "Do what it take to get the job done and forget the details" "Use it till it breaks, then buy a new one." Time is of the essence, Get it done, the details will take care of themselves." (III, 2011)\

This thinking is not cost effective in the long run. Yes! Money is of the essence. Yes! Time is of the essence. However by taking time to do it the right way the first time saves money and time in the long run. Yes, a little more money may be spent up front and more time is spent in the beginning. However you save time and money in the long run because the details have been thought out in full. Then you know what is really needed to do the job right.

Encarta World English Dictionary defines "**If**" as;

1.conj **used in indirect questions:** used in indirect speech to introduce a question that in direct speech requires the answer "yes" or "no"

"Asked if I would stay"

2. Conj **modifying statement:** used to indicate a modification to a statement, usually to add something negative or to indicate that there is less of something than originally expected

"A gallant, if misguided, attempt" "By Thursday, if not earlier"

3. Conj **introducing exclamation:** used to introduce an exclamation expressing surprise or dismay

"If that isn't the last straw!"

4. NOUN **doubt:** a doubt or uncertainty

"The proposal contains too many ifs for us to be enthusiastic about it."

5. NOUN **condition:** a condition or qualification

"I'm not very happy about the "ifs" written into the contract."

However the Phrase used most often is, "IF it happens I will deal with it at that point." Another phrase is "Don't worry about that now! If we come across it, we will deal with it at that point." (III, 2011)

 The facts are that in most cases the problem gets bigger and more hurtful. At that point you have to spend more effort to solve those problems. Very few problems will work themselves out on their own. There are a few but these will do so because someone is thoughtfully taking care of the small details as the project goes on.

Regardless of what the dictionary will say about these two words people in general use them to take short cuts that result in more problems or to set aside a problem till later. Later is in most cases, to late when it comes.

If you work for a company or own the company, you and the other employees need to show the customer that the company and its personnel care about the products and the equipment that is being used. The company is visible 24-7 all year long even if the personnel are not. Anything with a company logo on it is seen day in and day out.

In order for the public to perceive that the company is doing its job, it has to look and act the part even when the doors are closed. You may not see what or why a problem happens until after the fact but the public will. It is not "**IF**" a problem will happen but "**When**".

When a problem happens are you ready? You never set aside a problem or discount any fact for expediency. **It is not** the big picture that counts. It is the whole picture that counts and every detail there in. Everything has equal value.

The proper Idiom to use is.

"STAND BACK FARE ENOUGH TO SEE THE FOREST AND CLOSE ENOUGH TO SEE THE TREES."

You are a part of the problem and you are a part of the solution. From the CEO to the everyday employee everyone counts. All Ideas are valid regardless of who came up with them.

The reasons why things are to be done right the first time are varied. But I will state the most obvious one that I feel are of importance. These are ---

1. Company and personal visibility.
2. Fewer problems later.
3. Customer/public notice.
4. Personal feeling of an accomplishment well done.

Points 1 and 2 are of great importance. It does not take much effort to stop for a minute or two and visualize the equipment or product to be used. It is necessary to see the problems that will occur when it goes out into the field. When you see a problem deal with it, then you can prevent it from happening. You should do this every chance you have. This does not take a major leap of effort. Stop the problem before it happens. If this is not done the problem can only magnify and become worse. Then it will take a major effort in time and money to correct the problem.

Case in point:

One of the competitors to my company was delivering an ammonia nurse tank to a farmer. The driver lost control of the truck and rolled the tank. Fortunately no product was lost and no major injury happened. The driver was new to the area and not sure of the road traveled and was traveling at a high rate of speed. This employee came up on small short S curve with a little wooden creek bridge in the middle of it. He could not stop in time and lost it.

The nurse tank was rolled and the bottle separated from the carriage. One point of encouragement the tank was new and the tank held its integrity.

Points 1 and 3 are related but they stand on their own. Expedience is something that the public at large does not want to see or hear. The public is very fickle. If they see Products or equipment that is not in top shape they won't do business with you. There visual opinion of you and your company will make the difference in how they do business with you. I have personally witnessed a customer choose an old well maintained pump and motor over a new one for his use. It had nothing to do with price because the use of these units was and is a premium for the use to the farmer. Visually the well maintained unit was more appealing than the new one. There for the farmer felt that it would give him less worries while in his use. He saw that an effort was made to make it look good. When he pulled the starting rope and kicked off on the first pull, his mind was made up.

It made me, feel good, because I had reworked and put an effort into that units operation and visual appeal. Expedience is not an option when doing any job. Expedience is a job killer. When expedience is used too many times it will kill a business and jobs are lost. I have actually heard people say several times during my life "Get it put together and get it out and get on to the next one. I don't care what it looks like just get it out." The Customer has to perceive that it is going to work right and it is appealing to his eye. Otherwise you lose business.

The forth point is not only for the company but for you. If you have made the effort to, "DOT" every "I" and" CROSS" every "T" then you will have the feeling of a job well done. This is a good thing because most of the time this is the only credit you will receive other than a comment by the customer or a co-worker of how well the job was done or how good it looked and operated. It will not take long, if the company is on its toes, to look to you in a favorable way down the line. It does not happen right away or all the time but eventually you will be complemented because the public will notice the good or as it happens most of the time, the bad job being done. It will reflect either way on the company at large. If the company looks good you will look good and vice a versa.

In the following pages I am going to take on one project and walk through it. The steps can be applied to any project because it visualizes a complete and finished project taken to the nth' degree.

Do things in a set manor of operation. Keep this set manor in mind. You want to make sure when the unit or product goes out, they do not fail to do the job and stay in the field as long as possible without incident,

The points I make I feel are universal. These points are—

1. Look at the situation or equipment and try to discern the problems that can happen.

2. Put your hands on it and walk through the prescribed operation and check all the functions.

3. All details have equal weight. None are minor.

4. Discount nothing.

Point #1: Look at the situation or equipment and try to discern the problems that can happen.

I work in the farming industry for a division of a major national company. My area is in the distribution of Fertilizers and chemicals at the farm level or in proper terms an Agronomy distribution point.

I see a common enemy, namely **RUST.** The reason for the rust is Liquid fertilizer. The most common part of liquid fertilizer is nitrogen. Nitrogen is a sticky substance that will adhere to metal. Nitrogen is a very corrosive substance. As Nitrogen sit on the surface of most metals it causes a reaction between the metal and water. Any water! The water that is mixed with the nitrogen as it is applied to the fields or water that is found in the air around it. I have seen pumps and motors go out new with no problems and come back in 6mo. to a year later looking like a ball of rust. Then it took a major overhaul to put the unit back into service. The liquid fertilizer is spilled on the engine in the course of operation. Steps can be taken to lessen the exposure. The things I do to the engines and pumps may seem to be a little overkill but in the end it works and it works well.

(Figure 1) (Engines, 2011)

2. Put your hands on it and walk through the prescribed operation to check function. Figure 1 is an engine that was put into the field new and unprotected; it was out for about a year being used by four farmers without any minor upkeep. Then the liquid trailer was brought back to the shop with the engine and pump looking as you see it in figure 1. By far this is not a bad looking engine. I have actually seen worse, if you look at the connector bracket, (down arrow), between the engine and the pump you will see that it is badly rusted. I have seen these brackets so badly rusted that they could not be separated without breaking.

The first thing that is needed to be done is to take stock of all the damage. In this case, other than the appearance, the motor or pump was seized. To find out if the pump was or the motor was seized the pump and motor has to be separated. Once separated just pull the starting rope and turning the pump shaft to see which is seized. In this case the pump was seized.

Next both engine and pump need to be disassembled and cleaned. At this point the question is asked "why take the engine apart?" You do not need to disassemble the internal parts of the engine. All that is needed there is to check and change the oil if need be and refuel adding fuel stabilizer to the gas. But do pull the spark plug and check the gap and the condition of the plug its self. Clean or replace if it is necessary.

The main reason you disassemble the external parts of the engine is because of the <u>Health and Well Being of You and the Farmer.</u> Rust can cause *deterioration* of thin metal areas that can cut you or a farmer. Figures 2 and 3 are an example of this type of thing. The edges of the heat plates are not very well finished and can cut easily. If rust is added this type of cut can lead to a medical condition called lock jaw or tetanus. The Tetanus Virus thrives in rusty and dirty areas like this. (Medicine, last updated on 11 July 2010) The type of fever and body aches, associated with this disease are not what you want to have and it can lead to death.

(Figure 2)   (Figure

(Figure 4) (Industries)

The best way to prevent this in the future is to clean and paint if possible with a good quality rust and chemical resistant paint. Many of the spray paints on the market have this ability.

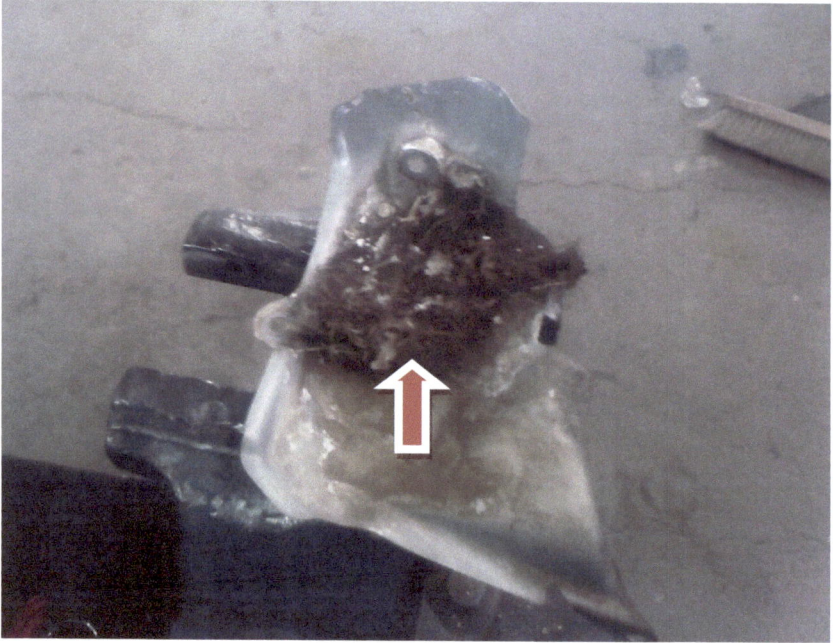

(Figure 5)

. Rodents often get into the small cavities of the engine. You will find them behind the heat plates and recoil units. There these rodents will hide from predators or build their nests. These rodents will die and lay there. Every time you start the engine the dead cells of the rodent will be thrown into the air along with any microbe that is on the carcass, Figure 5. Have you ever heard of Hantavirus? Hantavirus Pulmonary Syndrome (HPS), this is a disease that is caused by breathing in the air born rodent particles. The churning of the engine will toss them into the air for you to breath. Don't take a chance, this is a disease that can and has killed. (Medicine, last updated on 11 July 2010)

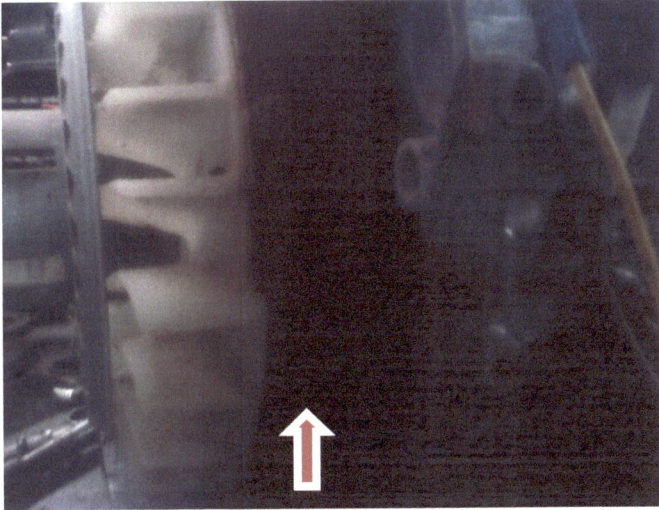

(Figure 6)

(Figure 7)

Another reason is that rust stops or slows electrical conductivity. There are places that you do not want electrical conductivity in the form of static charge, I will go into this later The fly wheel,(figure 6) under the recoil housing can rust and it is rust that can cause problems between the fly wheel and the pickups points of the coil,(Figure 7). Lightly buffing with a wire wheel will remove the rust. I pant the outer surfaces but do not paint the contact points as indicated by the arrows

Rust can invade any place moisture can get to. Any unprotected area is susceptible. In figure8 the outer foam filter was missing and Rust was present as well. Sometimes a light buffing of the surface to remove the rust is required. Then coat the metal area on top and bottom but not the middle section with a good non porous, rust inhibitor type primer and replace the foam outer filter. As the before and after photo, figure 9. Making this effort will help extend the life of the filter.

(Figure 8)

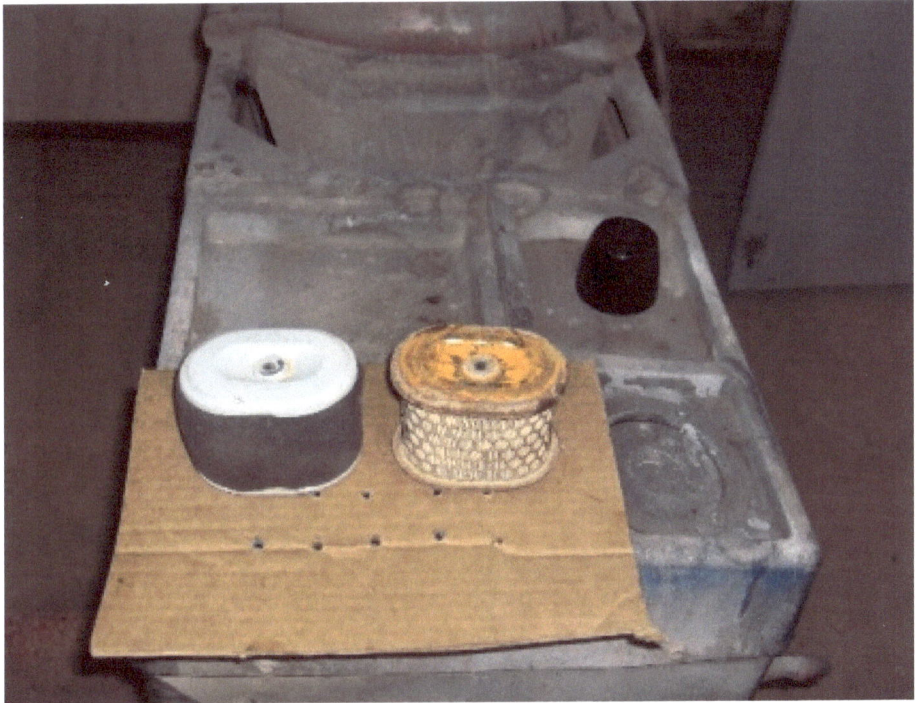

(Figure 9)

These two filters were just as bad when they came in from the field. After a light buffing, a coat of primer and a new foam filter it is as good as new. The cost of cleaning an old filter unit and replacing the foam filter is about a third of the cost of replacing a complete filter system.

(Figure 10)

The muffler of the engine is another expensive part. The more it is left unprotected the more deterioration there is. Do not take the Muffler apart. The screws are seated in place. Just lightly buff the outside areas and coat with a heat resistant pant. I choose a black paint that is resistant from 500 to 800 degrees F. The Idea here is to coat as much of the surface as possible. The one thing to know is when metal is heated it drives moisture away. As the metal cools it will attract moisture like a magnet. The partials of moisture may not be visible to the naked eye but it is there. use a heat gun and heat the surface to drive out the moisture and let the paint cool it down and seal the surface off.

3. All details have equal weight. None are minor.

I was an aviation electrician class A in the US Navy. The one thing that was stated many times was static charge; this is the unwanted electrical charge between two conductive metals. Similar and dissembler metals that can carry a charge will discharge a static charge.

(Figure 11)

Notice if you will the area inside the ring around the shaft. The gray specks you see is corrosion cause by electro static discharge. I have seen static electricity eat through the metal.

(Figure 1)

Remember figure 1? The adaptor plate is made of cast steel. The engine face it is attached to is aluminum. Dissimilar metals that conduct electricity. The metal adaptor plate in figure 11 for some reason had the gasket left off in assembly. The problem was easily solved because I had a used gasket. Using it as a template I made a gasket from a rubber inner tube, Shone in figure 12 and 13.

(Figure 12)

(Figure 13)

If you have to make a gasket do so, it will save money in the long run, namely replacement of the engine.

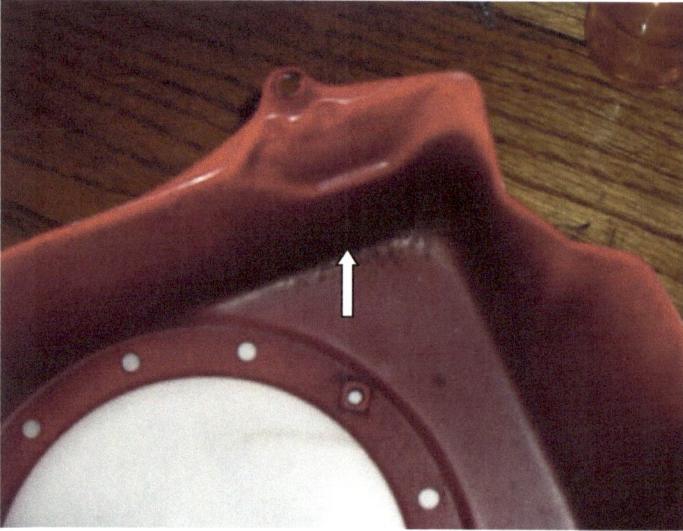

(Figure 14)

The inside areas of the recoil housing are susceptible to rust due to moisture and dirt. As well as the chemicals use in the agronomy industry. Figure 14 show the starting of rust in the corner of the recoil housing and Figure 15 show rust on the outside. I have seen it so bad that the rust had eaten through the metal. A light buffing here and coating with a good primer and appropriate color paint will solve this problem.

(Figure 15)

(Figure 16)

The pump and adapter bracket are most susceptible to rust. These two items come from the factory with only an anodized coating. This coating will not last very long in the field and is not resistant to most chemicals. By coating these two items with a good primer and color paint you will limit if not eliminate the rust problem for a long while. I use both a primer and paint because it gives a two layer barrier between the metal and the chemicals used. I use a dark blue for the 2" pumps and a dark green for the 3" pumps. This is to separate the sizes and make inventory easer. There are in the industry 1000, 1200, 1500, 1600 gallon liquid trailers. The size pump on each of them will vary. Here is where the Term "Expedience" comes into play. In many cases it does not matter what size pump is to be used! So when a pump and motor fail a quick replacement is made. That is, whatever size pump is available is used to replace the bad one. This will make a pump inventory a night mare. A good color code will ease the frustration of knowing which is which.

Also there is a danger in these motor pump unions. That is in the adaptor plate. The engine and pump shafts join in the adaptor plate and is in the open and can be touched. When in operation it should not be touched. This is because a finger can be lost or damaged if fingers are placed there during operation. I have seen people slip and try to catch hold of the pump or engine to prevent the fall. I paint the adaptor plate a bright read to warn everyone of the danger as in figure 17.

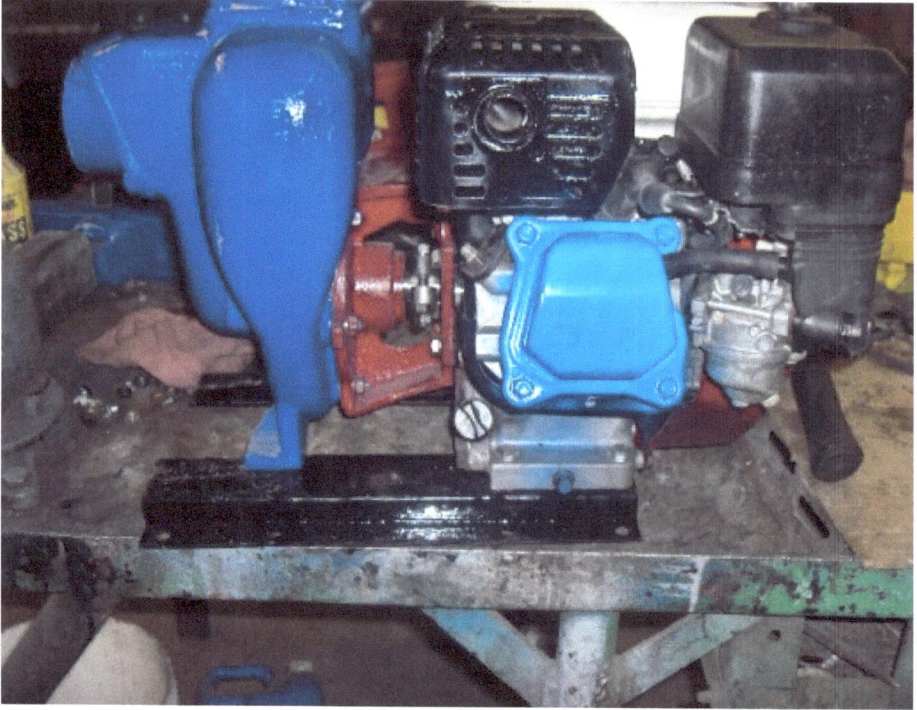

(Figure 17)

Point 3.Customer and/public notice is a big point. If there is a problem the customer will let you know. If there is one thing that is not wanted is an irate customer. By simply taking your time and going over each part and checking out everything can preempt problems. Some problems cannot be foreseen, like a rock being sucked up into the pump or an engine shelling out. But these problems can be lessened by placing filters in the lines and proper maintenance by changing the oil at regular intervals. It is important to take your time and think it through. Make a list of the things that you see that are wrong. Add to the list normal maintenance procedures. It is better to take care of the normal maintenance procedures when the unit is down than make time for scheduled maintenance unnecessarily at a later date. Once done it is out of the way, Till the next scheduled maintenance or the next breakdown.

Point 4. The Personal feeling of accomplishment for job done right. Doing the job right and knowing it, is one thing that makes it easier to do the next job. A personal goal or achievement that can show the corporate leaders you care and can do the job. Besides which of the following is better for the company image and you.

(Figure1)

OR

(Figure 17)

Which heat plate would you use?

OR

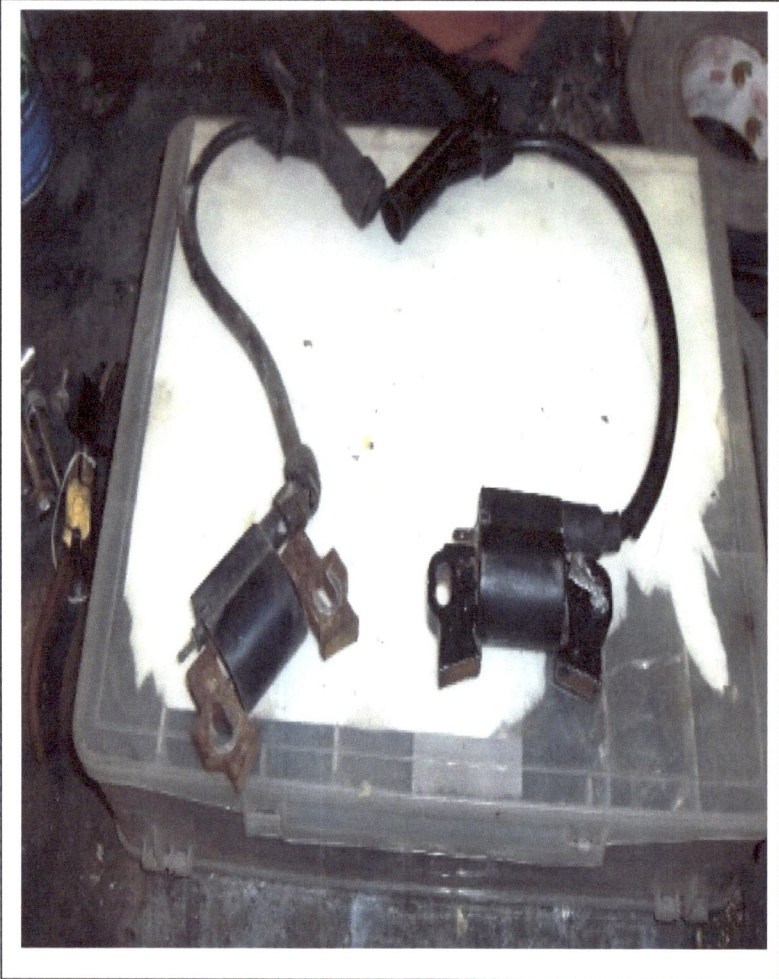

Which Coil would you use?

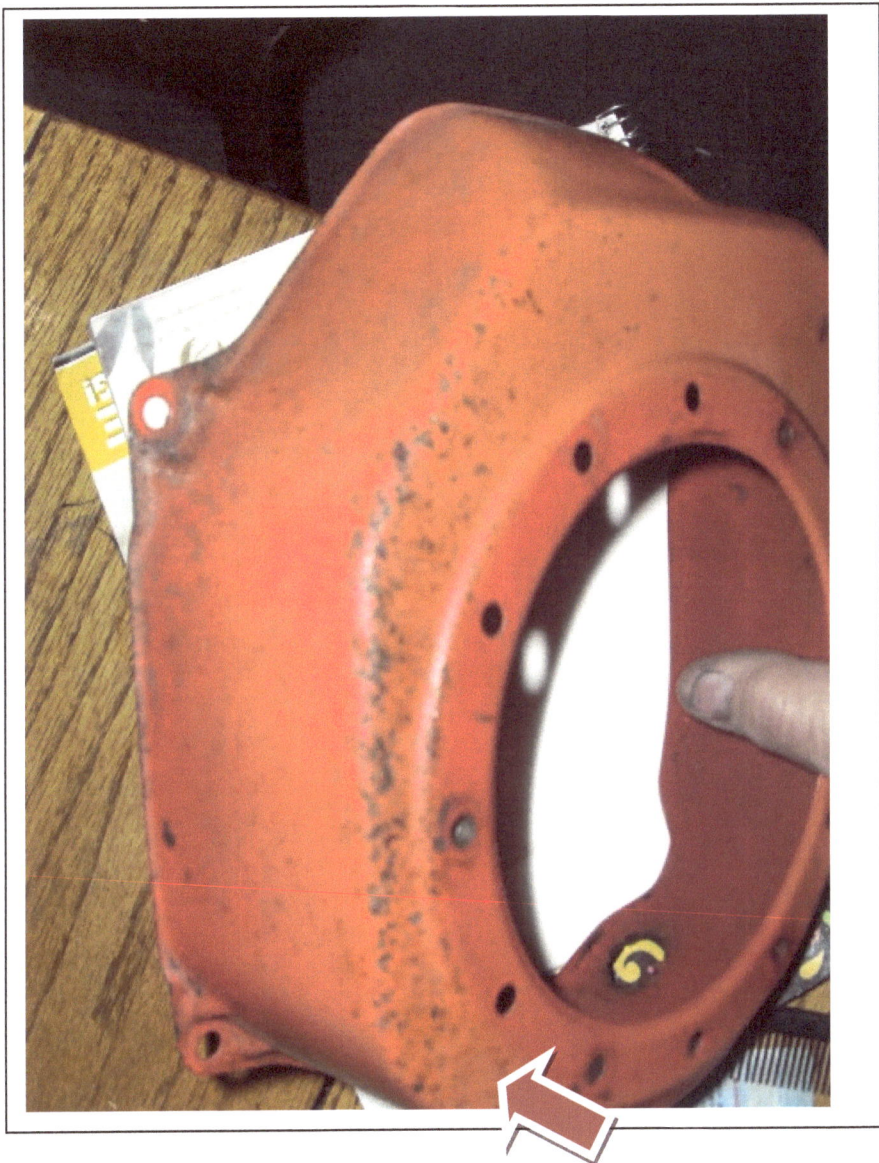

Which Fly wheel housing is better?   This one?

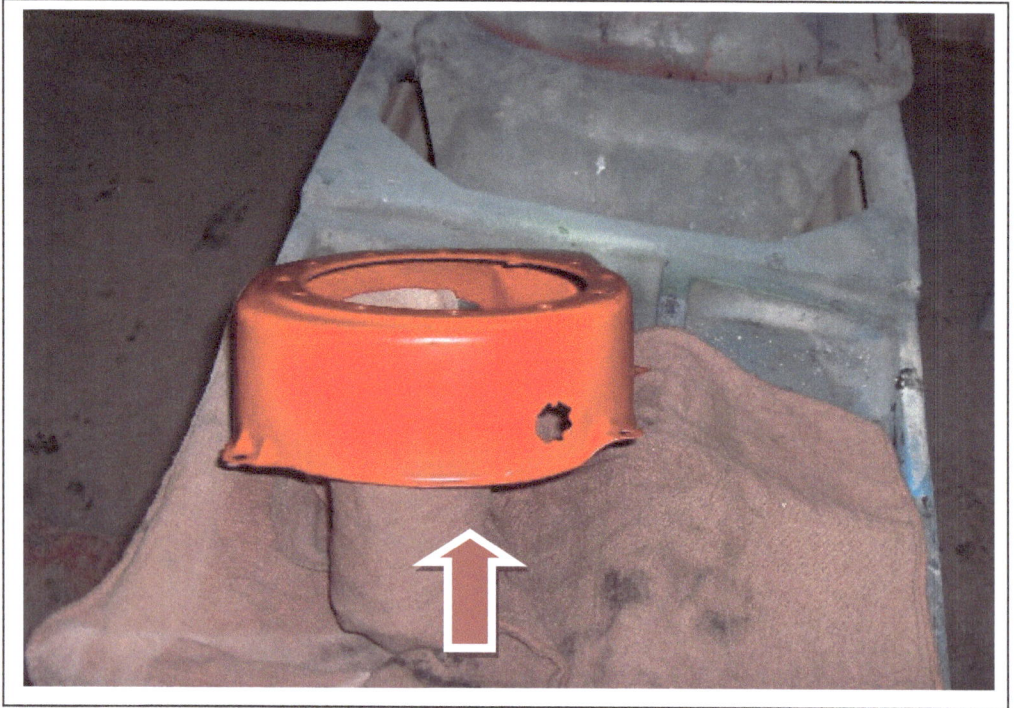

Or, this one?

And so on and so on

You are the beginning and the end of any effort that can be made. IT starts with you. Remember

"It is done when all avenues are explored and problems repaired or fixed, no matter how long it takes." It will save money and time in the long run.

REFERENCES:

Encarta World English Dictionary,Online. (2011). Encarta.

Engines, H. S. (2011). Honda Small Engine Internet sight. *Engine.Honda.com* , ?

III, C. M. (2011). *My Life.* USA: ME.

Industries, T. 21400 Northwest Freeway, Cypress, Texas 77429: internet sight.

Medicine, U. N. (last updated on 11 July 2010). *Medline plus.* Oneline medical dictionary: U.S. National Library of Medicine.

sight, I. (2010 & 2011). United Plains Ag. *Internet sight* , 40.

www.ingramcontent.com/pod-product-compliance
Lightning Source LLC
Chambersburg PA
CBHW041711200326
41518CB00001B/157